BUY LOW, RENT HIGH

LEGAL NOTICES

The information presented herein represents the view of the authors as of the date of publication. Because of the rate with which conditions change, the author reserves the right to alter and update his opinion based on the new conditions. This book is for informational purposes only. While every attempt has been made to verify the information provided in this book, neither the authors nor their affiliates/partners assume any responsibility for errors, inaccuracies or omissions. Any slights of people or organisations are unintentional. You should be aware of any laws which govern business transactions or other business practices in your country and state. Any reference to any person or business whether living or dead is purely coincidental.

Every effort has been made to accurately represent this product and its potential. Examples in these materials are not to be interpreted as a promise or guarantee of earnings. Earning potential is entirely dependent on the person using our product, ideas and techniques. We do not purport this as a "get rich scheme."

Your level of success in attaining the results claimed in our materials depends on the time you devote to the program, ideas and techniques mentioned your finances, knowledge and various skills. Since these factors differ according to individuals, we cannot guarantee your success or income level. Nor are we responsible for any of your actions.

Any and all forward looking statements here or on any of our sales material are intended to express our opinion of earnings potential. Many factors will be important in determining your actual results and no guarantees are made that you will achieve results similar to ours or anybody else's, in fact no guarantees are made that you will achieve any results from our ideas and techniques in our material.

CONTENTS

BUY LOW RENT HIGH

*How anyone can be financially free in
the next 12 months
by investing in property*

Samuel Leeds

INTRODUCTION

Somebody once said that you are just a book away from the knowledge you need that can change your finances, change your future and change your life.

I want to congratulate you for taking the time to read this book. Most people fail because of lack of knowledge and I trust that as we journey together throughout this process you will experience massive results and revolutionise your life. Although this book is about property investing, it is actually about you. Property is just a vehicle that will ultimately be able to take you to the places where you want to go.

By the time you finish reading this book, you will understand more about property investing than most professional property investors. You will know all the best areas in which to invest and what kind of properties will make you the most money. You will understand how to set up a House of Multiple Occupancy (HMO) property and even how to buy it without any money. You will have mastered many creative strategies, such as Lease Option Agreements, deal sourcing, and how to formulate like a pro.

Read this book and apply it, and there is no reason why you cannot build a £1 million portfolio and become financially free in the next year or two, even if you currently have nothing.

WHO THE HECK AM I?

I began learning all about property investment in 2007, just before I'd even left school. I had no money and couldn't get a mortgage because of my age. By the age of 21, I was financially free, and in the following year I had a portfolio worth over £1,000,000.

Since then, I've taught thousands of people how to do the same and in the last twelve months alone, I've sourced in excess of 100 properties in the UK for some of my students.

Since gaining my financial freedom, I've set up a large national network that supports Christians in business, as well as starting up Good News All Round, an organisation that brings clothes and clean water to people living in severe poverty in developing countries.

CHAPTER 1

This is my mission

Educate yourself

My dad was a professional magician and he taught me how to entertain with comedy magic. During my time at school, it was assumed that I would eventually follow in his footsteps and that we would work together. He's a very intelligent man and has always been able to make a living for himself. He's the kind of guy who could travel the world while finding opportunities to make enough money to pay for his trip. I love my dad and have learnt a lot from him, and still do. When leaving school, I began working for him and although on the whole it was fun, deep down I wanted more with my life.

Shortly after starting my new career as an entertainer, I had a very spiritual experience and felt a calling on my life to travel the world, help the poor and set up my own business. I began to go to church regularly and that year I was given a book by a man who subsequently became my mentor. The name of the book was *Rich Dad Poor Dad* written by Robert Kiyosaki.

The story of *Rich Dad Poor Dad* was about a boy who had a loving, hardworking father who didn't know much about investing or property. Instead, he had a normal job and he taught his son to follow after him. But the son had another 'father', who was actually more like a mentor to him. This father was financially literate and knew all about investing, property and economics. The boy decided to follow his other father's advice and as a result he became extremely rich.

It was a great book and completely opened my eyes to the world of passive income and property investing. It was quite ironic because I had recently left working for my dad and was now looking for a mentor. My new mentor spent hours talking to me about my dreams and he believed in me. He himself had recently been on a property investment course with Simon Zutshi and encouraged me to do the same. It turned out that Simon also used to be a magician but had quit and was running a very successful property investment business.

I loved the idea of property investing. I'd built up £6,000 worth of savings from delivering around 42,000 newspapers over a four year period while a schoolboy. I asked my mentor what I should do next and he responded,

"Educate yourself."

This was probably the best advice I have ever received. I could have spent the £6,000 towards buying a house, but instead I spent the whole amount and more on educating myself. I attended some courses that were useless and others that were outstanding. Simon Zutshi was extremely generous and helpful and I certainly wouldn't be where I am today if it wasn't for him. I went along to a Property Investors Network which Simon was running in Birmingham. All my other friends were just starting college and here I was mingling with these middle-aged property investors. Afterwards, I had a good chat with Simon and he was very helpful, but more importantly, he believed in me. A short time later, Simon called me to ask how things were going. I told him that I had no money and was too young to even get a mortgage, so despite being extremely excited about property, it was probably just a pipe dream.

Simon told me straight that this business was for anybody and spent 45 minutes giving me encouragement over the phone. Today, Simon and I are still friends and I will always have gratitude in my heart for both my mentor and Simon Zutshi for believing in me.

This was in 2008 just before the recession. The strategy was to buy properties at 20 per cent Below Market Value (BMV) and then quickly refinance them to their true value. This resulted in getting the deposit money back and, ultimately, leaving you with a 'No Money Down Deal' (more on that later).

Despite not being able to get a mortgage, I began helping my mentor source properties and he agreed that if I was successful, when I turned 18 years of age he would host a mortgage for me, which meant I could get a property of my own.

That year was one of the best years of my life. I quit my career of just three months working in my dad's entertainment company; I had a spiritual experience that led me to plugging into my local church; I learned to drive and bought a car; I attended every property investors programme I could; and networked like a madman. I sourced as many properties as possible and made friends with estate agents in about ten different cities across the UK. That year, my mentor managed to get five No Money Down Deals while also investing in apartments from the equity pulled from his own home. We were smashing it!

My mentor bought a House of Multiple Occupation (HMO) property close to Bournville, Birmingham. He had employed a builder to do the conversion, costing around £45,000, but the builder ended up charging lots of extras and it was quite a difficult time.

I began searching for more properties in the Bournville area and would offer 20 per cent BMV on everything I saw until somebody said yes. Three months before my 18th birthday came an opportunity to buy a 3-bed house for £100,000. The value was £120,000 and if I was to use the method I had been learning, it could be a No Money Down Deal.

The condition of the house was good and it had an extra reception room, so potentially it could be a multi-let house. The deal was completed three weeks before my 18th birthday. I was absolutely over the moon! Not only had a bought a house before the age of 18, but I was set to do it again and again.

This property was giving me a profit just shy of £1,000 per month and has done so ever since. I was still living at home and had very few over-heads. I was also making extra money by sourcing properties for my mentor and finding tenants for the other investors with whom I had become friends.

Discipline your disappointment

After buying my first 'No Money Down' property I was ready to go again and found my next perfect property. However, just three days before we were due to exchange contracts I received a bad phone call. The mortgage company that I had lined up ready for the deal, Mortgage Express, were about to close their firm. In fact, the whole method of buying and remortgaging was no longer possible as lenders were now scared to lend. The credit crunch was coming and it was coming big!

I was absolutely gutted. All these expensive courses, all these dreams, gone!

I had always been trained to celebrate my suc-cess, but I had not yet mastered the art of disci-plining my disappointment. Everybody went into a frenzy and many investors jumped ship.

The days of buying property with no money were over ... apparently.

I went on a programme called the Millionaire Mind Intensive. It was incredible and I learned all about money and passive income, but more importantly, I learned about myself. I learned that I was responsible for my success and there are endless possibilities to be creative. I learned that it wasn't about the economy or the rules – my results were down to me.

I attended endless personal development programmes, became very well read and practised martial arts with my Wing Chun teacher. I developed a great respect for Jim Rohn, who sadly passed away shortly before I discovered his work.

Jim said,

"The same wind blows on us all but it is the setting of the sail that determines our destination."

With this new mindset, alongside my property knowledge and ongoing training, I learned about Lease Option Agreements, raising finance and other creative ways, all of which enabled me to buy more property and become financially free by the age of 21.

Today, I earn a six-figure residual income, along-side all the growing equity in my £1 million port-folio. I am set to become an automatic multi-millionaire by the age of 30. I say this not to boast of myself, but to boast of the strategies that I will be teaching in this book.

You may lose friends

Although I was making good money for an 18 year old, it was never about the money but about what the money could do. My church was often talking about 'lack of resources' which limited the work they could do and I knew that I could help.

On one occasion, an Indian missionary visited our church to speak about his work in Punjab. They were building orphanages for children and giving hope to the poorest of the poor in many practical and spiritual ways. Mukhtiar couldn't speak very good English, but his words broke my heart. After he finished his talk, I asked if I could pray with him and he invited me to visit the work in Punjab. I agreed without a second's thought and ended up working with him for two weeks. It was life changing. The more money I would make, the more I wanted to travel and help the less fortunate. I went to India, Zambia, Kenya and Tanzania, working alongside charities that help the poor and give hope to the hopeless. I climbed to the top of Mount Kilimanjaro and raised thousands for Compassion UK and decided that I wanted to set up my own charity one day.

In September 2011, I was in a position where I could stop working altogether and signed up to Bible college full-time. My plan was to spend three years studying theology and training for the ministry and then become a minister in the church. My church was my family and I loved everyone dearly and wanted to work alongside my pastor who was like a spiritual father to me.

My spiritual mentors began to have 'quiet words' with me about money. They warned me that money brings problems and I had to make a decision – God or money. This troubled me as I felt compelled to be a successful investor and entrepreneur. My heart was to help people but I questioned myself because lots of their teaching and sermons were about the poor being blessed and the rich being greedy.

While at college I began studying the Bible's teaching about money and possessions and wrote a dissertation on biblical economics. I came to the conclusion that money is just a tool and as long as you are generous and hold it loosely, it's a very good tool that can bring a lot of positive change, both in your personal life and in the life of others around you.

I began to feel like a rebel and felt distanced from my church and college which hurt me a lot. My pastor told me that I was arrogant and needed humility. He told me to submit to the church properly and stop running ahead with my overly zealous visions. I told him I wouldn't.

I said,

"Pastor, I love you and respect you. However, I will not stop doing what I believe God has called me to do."

As a result he got very annoyed and dismissed me from the meeting.

After weeks of awkwardness and feeling unwelcome at church, I left alone, I felt betrayed. I wanted my family back. I wanted things to be like they used to be. I continued to persist and hoped it would blow over and they would see that my heart is good. I arrived at one evening service and one of the elders stood in front of the door. My heart sank and I asked,

"Are you stopping me from coming inside?"

He responded,

"It's best you leave, sorry."

That's the last time I have ever been to that church and nearly all of my friends from there have refused to speak to me.

After this awful experience of being completely misunderstood and kicked out of the church, I realised that it was not their fault. The people who had opposed me simply had a twisted view of money and were taking it out on me. I have nothing but love for every single person who gave me a hard time and if it were not for them I would not have the strength I have now.

It forced me to study economics, scripture and philosophy, but most of all, myself.

Why do I teach?

Since then, I have joined another church who accept and embrace me. I have also set up a Christian Business Network where we support Christians to be successful in business practically and emotionally. It has become my mission to release people from the guilt of success and teach all I know to equip them to be prosperous so that they can also help make the world a better place.

We have become a national organisation with ten branches across the UK and over 120 events every single year. The network is called Training Kings.

Growing this organisation has stretched me as a person and has led me to writing the best-selling book, *Do the Possible, Watch God Do the Impossible*. It has also given me the opportunity to speak at large Christian and business conferences across the globe.

The reason I am writing a book about property investing is because I want to leave a legacy after I'm gone. I want thousands of people to be able to say that they became financially independent and have been able to do extraordinary things with the time and money that property has given them. I believe wholeheartedly in the strategies I teach because they are tried and tested, but more importantly, I believe in you.

Some have asked me,

"Why do you teach about property investment when you can make so much more money investing in property?"

They have missed the point. Not everything I do is purely money driven. This is part of my mission.

So as I conclude this first chapter, I want to encourage you to think about your mission.

If it's just about the money, life will get pretty boring. When you have as much as you want and more, what will be the purpose of life for you?

I pray that your mission goes beyond money and goes beyond yourself.

CHAPTER 2

Now is the time to invest in property

The thing I love about property is that it is bricks and mortar. If you invest in the stock market you can lose everything and your investment can become worthless. Similarly, if you invest into a business that doesn't work you can lose a lot of money. However, with property, generally speaking, the worst thing that can happen is you have a bad tenant who loses you some rent or you have to carry out unexpected repairs to the property. The very worst case is probably needing to sell the house and starting from square one, but this is extremely unlikely, especially if you know what you are doing.

In order to work out what the future holds for the property market and the best time to invest, you need to look back at history. Although much of what I say applies to many countries, I am writing about the UK market, so any international readers please bear this in mind.

As far as we can recollect, after expansion comes recession, and after recession comes expansion. This is not my opinion, this is basic economic history. History tends to repeat itself.

From 2008 to 2014 we were in a pretty big recession. House prices fell or became stagnant and rents hardly moved in this period of time. In fact, rents have hardly moved from the year 2000. So what does this suggest? It suggests that probably sometime before 2025, house prices will rocket. More excitingly, it suggests that rents will go up drastically too.

A great time to invest is always after a big long recession, so I believe it's a very good time to buy at this very moment.

Some people are worried about interest rates rising and forcing mortgage payments to increase. You can currently fix your rates for up to 10 years; the only thing that is about to rocket up is house prices and rents! Let's get real.

Most people will always think of a reason why not to do something until it's too late and then they kick themselves. Please don't be one of those people. Be smart and start investing now.

As one smart person put it,

"Don't wait to buy property, buy property and wait."

What about after the expansion? Will house prices drop again?

On average, property prices double around every ten years. You can go back through history and see for yourself. This has been the case for about as far as we can see. Some will argue that it's every twelve years that prices double, but the bottom line is that they go up drastically over time.

Is property investing risky?

When I was at school, if I had told my teachers that I wanted to become a property investor they would have said that it was risky. They would have told me that if I wanted to guarantee success I needed to follow their system. I am sure you are familiar with it.

This is what success looks like:

1) Study hard at school as it's important you get good grades.

2) Go on to university if you want to be paid well.
3) Get a good job for life.
4) If you buy a house, pay off the mortgage as quickly as possible.
5) Save as much as you can to store away safely in the bank.
6) The harder you work the more money you'll make.
7) Look forward to retirement because that's the good life.

The truth is:

1) Most people do not benefit from good grades.
2) Most people who finish university still struggle to get a job.
3) A good job for life does not exist.
4) Paying off the mortgage quickly is not smart.
5) Your money is shrinking in the bank.
6) Some of the poorest people are the hardest workers.
7) If retirement is your motivation you will be extremely disappointed.

These lies have become so accepted in our society but they will lead you to working 40 hours per week for 40 years to retire on 40 per cent of what you struggled to live on in the first place. And that's me being generous! I meet many people now working 50/60 hours per week at a job they hate, just to earn a living. Somebody once said that a job stood for **J**ump **O**ut of **B**ed, on a **J**ourney **O**f **B**oredom, to be **J**ust **O**ver **B**roke and the sad part is that it's true for many people.

I have nothing against schools, jobs or banks. They have their place, but as Jim Rohn says,

"Formal education will earn you a living, but self-education will earn you a fortune."

Some people are offended with my perspective on this but I can only speak from my experience. I am not saying this to make anybody look or feel bad, but because I am on a mission to liberate as many people I can to be financially free and to live the lives they deserve. I am saying this from a position of love, not arrogance. There is nothing wrong with normal, but you read this book because you have greatness inside of you and are on your way to financial freedom.

Money depreciates in value

Banks are not set up to make you rich, but to make themselves rich.

Let's assume you work super hard at work and manage to put aside £50,000 worth of savings. You put that money in the bank while you decide how to best use it. Your accumulating interest is obviously very low from a traditional bank so you decide to wait a whole ten years before checking how much your money has accumulated.

Do you know how much your £50,000 would be worth after waiting for a decade?

Equivalent to approximately £35,000!

How so? Because as the cost of living goes up while the money stays the same, the money shrinks, it depreciates in value.

Let me give an example of this. Twenty years ago, if you were a millionaire it was a massive achievement. You were considered rich. Today, everybody seems to be a millionaire; it's no big deal. The reason is because £1 million today is worth a lot less than it was twenty or even ten years ago. In the very same way, your money in the bank is worth less month by month, year by year.

Property makes you rich

Let's now imagine you invested that same £50,000 into a house. We know that typically houses double in value every ten years or so, so after ten years your £50,000 should be worth around £100,000 right? Actually, no!

Unless you bought the house for cash, the £50,000 would typically be the deposit on the house. A £50,000 deposit should easily get you a buy-to-let property worth £200,000.

What doubles? The deposit money or the value of the house? The answer is that the value of the house doubles. So your £50,000 has now become £250,000 in over just ten years. That's a 40 per cent Return on Investment (ROI) every single year just for buying an average house.

We call this 'leverage' and this is why so many people get rich almost by accident through buying property.

You may think I am being unrealistic, but remember this is not my opinion. My calculations are based upon what's happened throughout recent history and history always repeats itself. Let's face it, even if your investment doubled after twenty years I am sure you'd still be pretty happy with that.

One of the things my mentor used to always say to me was,

"Capital growth does not pay the bills."

Knowing that your properties are going to sky-rocket in value over time and you will become wealthy one day through capital appreciation is pretty exciting. But you cannot sit around waiting for it to happen because we never know exactly when that will be.

However, I have some superb news. In property investment you get paid twice – once in capital growth and secondly in rental income.

Communism does not work

Imagine that as you've been reading this book, you've got super excited and before finishing the rest of the book you've blindly gone and bought a house. Let's assume you've just walked into your local estate agent and asked if you could buy the most recent property the agent has put on the market. Not only that, you're happy to pay the full asking price. It would be a silly thing to do, but let's do a case study to see the consequences.

Average property price: £150,000

Likely deposit: £37,500

Monthly mortgage payments: £375

Average monthly rent: £675

Other expenses: £75

Monthly profit: £225

This is just a rough estimation based on average figures in today's market. Average house prices in 2017 are around £150,000.

People in London hear this and say, "You wouldn't get a shed for that much", while my northern friends say with a surprised voice, "Do houses really exist that are that expensive!"

I'm based in the Midlands and I'm working on averages across the country.

Twenty-five per cent is a very standard amount to put down as a deposit.

I'm working on 4 per cent interest rates on an interest-only mortgage. My broker is currently fixing them at 2.5 per cent but I'm working on 4 per cent as I want this book to stay relevant and I'm aware that these things vary over time.

The average rent is £675 per month, but do remember this will go up with time too.

Monthly expenses are minimal but will include landlord insurance of around £180 per year, possibly management costs depending on how you manage it, and possibly some small maintenance costs from time to time. £75 per month is just an example, but this will vary depending on the house and the landlord.

So this will leave you in profit with an ROI of about 7 per cent. Not only would your house appreciate in value and make you rich, you are also making a nice passive income stream at the same time.

Let's compare this with the bank.

Average house

Total investment: £37,500
Annual profit: £2,700
Return on Investment: 7.2 per cent
Plus: CAPITAL GROWTH

Average bank

Total investment: £37,500
Annual profit: £187.50
Return on Investment: 0.5 per cent
Minus: DEPRECIATION

Please don't forget that this house was one you bought straight from an estate agent with zero thought or strategy and ultimately you would still make very good money from it. There would be some fees attached to buying any property but I hope I have made my point that even buying blind you will be a hundred times better off than putting your money into a bank. Later on, I will be explaining how you can buy a property for £100,000 and achieve a rent of £1,400 per month.

So, you could have the same two people with the same job who live in the same street.

Both of them work hard and save up £37,500.

Person A puts it in the bank.
Person B buys an average property at random.

Person A is broke, Person B is rich.

Jim Rohn says,

"I teach my kids to have two bicycles. One to ride and one to rent. How hard does it get with a little ingenuity?"

The trick to financial freedom

The trick to financial freedom is twofold:

1) Figure out what passive income is.
2) Accumulate enough passive income to cover your lifestyle.

Let me explain the difference between passive and active income.

Active income is the income that we are pro-grammed to make right from the time we leave school and go into the workplace. You work once and get paid once. This is basically trading your time for money.
Passive income is where you work once and get paid again and again. Passive income can be created from a systemised business, a franchise, network marketing or royalties, but most easily through property. How many times do you need to buy the house to keep getting the rent? The answer is just once, of course.

As much as I love the big income you can make through property by buying and selling, capital growth and all kinds of clever ways, my favourite is the income through rent because it is steady, painless and passive.

The definition of 'financial freedom' is when your passive income is equal to or greater than your living expenses.

The definition of 'ultimate financial freedom' is when your passive income is equal to or greater than your desired lifestyle.

I achieved financial freedom by the age of 21 not because I am super clever, but because it is actually pretty easy. I am now ultimately financially free but that has taken a little longer.

My question to you is how much passive income do you need to become financially free? Write it down and ingrain that figure in your brain. By the end of this book you will probably realise that you only need around three properties to become completely financially free.

CHAPTER 3

Choosing the right property

Formulas not feelings

Property investing is a business, so do not get emotionally attached when deciding what to buy. Your house is your product and your tenant is your customer.

In 2015, I did an experiment with 900 professional property investors and the results were astounding. I photographed two of my properties and showed them to the investors. I asked them if they had to buy one of the properties and they only had one question before buying it, what would the question be.

They looked intently at both properties. One was pretty with a lovely garden. The other was grey and ugly. Both were terraced properties. Ninety per cent of the investors asked, "How much are they selling for?" That was their first question.

The pretty one was selling for £110,000, the ugly one for £150,000.

I told them they didn't have to decide just yet, they could ask another question.

Seventy-five per cent of the investors then asked, "Where are they located?"

I told them. The pretty house for £110,000 is in County Durham. The ugly house for £150,000 is in Birmingham.

Based on the pictures and these two answers, I asked them which house would they buy if they had to choose right now. Sixty-five per cent said the pretty house in County Durham. The remaining 35 per cent said the ugly one in Birmingham.

I told them that they had one final question before deciding which one to buy. Of course, this was only an experiment and they would not actually be buying either, but most of the investors thought long and hard. They had one final question to ask before it was decision time.

Forty per cent of them asked miscellaneous questions such as, "Where is the nearest hospital?", "Is there a back garden?", "What are the neighbours like?", and so on.

Finally, the rest asked the question I had been waiting for all along. The number one question that you should be asking straight away. And that is ... "What is the rent!?"

The rent on the pretty house in Durham for £110,000 was £400 per month.

The rent on the ugly house in Birmingham for £150,000 was £1,500 per month.

I asked one last time, which one would you buy? At this point 100 per cent of the investors said they would buy the house in Birmingham, giving them £1,500 rental income.

The moral of this story is that even professional investors constantly look for the wrong things because of their emotions. This business is all about formulas and not about feelings.

The ugly houses are best

Your portfolio is not for show and you will rarely visit it, if at all. When I'm buying a house I don't care whatsoever what it looks like. I don't care about the driveway, the garden or the neighbour's dog. I don't care that much about where it is and how much it is going for as long as somebody is around to manage it and the rent is high enough to give me a nice return. If you remember nothing else in the chapter remember this – it is all about the rent!

I speak to so many people who are in the process of buying a property investment and I ask them,

"That's great! What are you buying?"

They respond,

"A place in Bristol."

When I ask why Bristol they go on to explain that their daughter is moving to Bristol University and they wanted to kill two birds with one stone. Commercially, this is absolutely crazy!

Please never try to kill two birds with one stone; please never buy when your emotions are involved.

In this example they would have been better off buying a good investment house in the right area and then just fund their daughter though Bristol University and have money left over at the end of it too!

Get with the times

When I started building my portfolio back in 2008, the only thing I was interested in was how Below Market Value (BMV) the deal was. If it was 20 per cent or more BMV, I would buy it.

This was great then because you could refinance it and pull your money out, but today that is much more complicated. Things became more difficult when lenders began requiring you to own the property for at least six months before you could refinance. This meant that the money you had put down for the property was tied up for six months or more, which became less viable for many investors.

The second problem was that valuers became more conservative, especially when you were trying to pull your money out. For example, if you were to find a house that was worth £150,000 and buy it for £115,000, not only would you have to wait six months to refinance it back up to its true value of £150,000 but when you did, the valuer would come out and say it was only worth £115,000, which is what you paid for it! Many investors would challenge the valuer and show the proof of its true value based on similar sold properties in the street but as far as the valuer was concerned you bought it for £115,000 six months ago so therefore that was its new true value.

If your strategy is to buy BMV to refinance and pull your money out, the only way this can be done is by adding value to the property. If you converted it into a commercial property, for example, and then proved to the valuer why it was now worth more, you could still potentially pull it off as a No Money Down Deal.

I will not be going into this because there is much to be considered and when you are relying on builders sticking to budget and valuers being in a good mood, it can be very stressful and can go wrong.

I like to play it safe myself and especially only like to teach things that are safe because if somebody read this book, took action and lost a lot of money I would feel awful.

Sometimes investors want BMV properties for other reasons. It may be that they want to buy it cheap and sell it on. If you watch some of the property shows they make it look all so romantic. Buy a cheap run-down house, renovate it and then sell it on to make a small fortune before do-ing it again. This strategy has its place but in my opinion it is risky and time-consuming and we are just not in the right market for this right now.

There are new and even simpler ways to buy a property without using any money which I will be teaching later on in this book, but the reason for me explaining this is because some investors are still stuck in the 2008 mindset of 'BMV is everything'. Today, I don't care if it's BMV or not, all I care about is my rent because that is what will give me my high Return on Investment (ROI) and that is what will bring me my passive in-come.

Don't be an idiot

I had a phone call in May 2016 from Tanya, an estate agent from whom I had bought a few houses the year before. Tanya sounded frustrated but pleased I had answered the call. She explained that there was this 'professional investor', let's call him Steve. Steve had viewed and placed offers on 200 properties, all with agents and all in Wolverhampton. Every offer had been 20 per cent below the asking price and every single offer had been rejected. She asked me if I could have a word with Steve as he was upsetting hundreds of vendors and killing his reputation with her branch and many other estate agents. I told Tanya to ask Steve to attend my Property Investors Crash Course. I'm running my next course and guess who turns up? Steve!

I welcomed him and he told me with a firm voice,

"I have now found my perfect deal which is 20 per cent BMV, but I thought I would come anyway just to see what it's all about."

I smiled and told him I was glad he had made the effort to come down.

Two hours into the programme, Steve realised that his 'perfect property' was actually a terrible investment and he was ready to withdraw from his offer. Four hours into the programme Steve worked out that he could actually buy two properties with his deposit money. Eight hours into the programme Steve had found these two properties and was ready to buy. Within three months Steve had the keys to two new houses that now make him a full-time income. He is now sourcing deals and living a life he never imagined was possible.

The BMV trap

Let me show you the figures. Please note that Steve had a total of £58,000 to invest when we met.

Here's Steve's dream investment that took him 500 hours to find:

Asking price: £190,000
Agreed sale: £152,000
Renovation: £10,000
Monthly mortgage payments: £335
Monthly rent: £700

In Steve's mind this was an incredible deal. He had three options:

1) Refinance it and pull some of his money out.
2) Rent it out and make a profit of £365 per month which would be a 9 per cent ROI.
3) Buy and sell and make at least £30,000.

Doesn't this sound like a great deal? Let me explain why Steve pulled out.

1) Just because the asking price is £190,000 it doesn't mean that this is the true value. After doing some research on the course he discovered that it is actually only worth £172,000.
2) Refinancing after a light £10,000 refurbishment is just not going to happen. All the money you put into this deal is staying there
3) You could buy it and sell it for £172,000 but there is now only £20,000 to play with, not £40,000. By the time you have paid your legal fees both when buying and selling, plus estate agent fees and stamp duty, you would be left with around £10,000 profit, assuming all went to plan. That is a lot of work for such a small amount of profit with no guarantees.
4) You could rent it out and get 9 per cent ROI. In reality, it would be slightly less but even so, I am not getting excited.

Now let's compare this with what Steve ended up actually buying. The properties were both pretty much identical and in the same area, so I will just outline one of the two properties he bought.

Here are Steve's new deals – these took less than one day to find:

Asking price: £85,000
Market value: £87,000
Agreed sale: £85,000
Renovation: £6,000
Monthly mortgage payments: £185
Bills: £300
Monthly rent: £1350

Because this property is so much cheaper, Steve was able to source and buy two of these deals using his £58,000 worth of savings.

Conveniently, they are both located within two miles from his own home so he manages them himself and they are both giving him a cashflow of £865 per month. That's a total of £1,730 per month. For some people this alone would mean financial freedom.

Does it matter that these properties were not BMV? Of course not!

What kind of properties were they? Multi-lets.

Where are these kinds of deals? Everywhere.

CHAPTER 4

Houses of Multiple Occupancy (HMOs)

The first thing you should look for when deciding what kind of property to buy is one with a high rent. How do you get such a high rent? The easiest way is to rent a property out on a room-by-room basis. This type of property is known as a multi-let or a House of Multiple Occupation (HMO).

Most investors who buy HMOs go about it in a completely wrong way. I was one of them and in this chapter I'll share my experience and in doing so, I reckon that I'll save many of you at least £30,000 per deal.

Make sure you're within the law

In today's market – 2017 – if a property is over three floors or more, with five or more tenants, you will need to license this as an official HMO.

If it is a smaller HMO, with four or fewer people, or if it is just over two floors, typically this will be referred to as a multi-let. You should not need planning permission for an HMO unless there are seven or more separate tenants. The rules do change from time to time, so it's important to do your own research before buying any property.

Councils will potentially insist that all rental properties have a license and this scares many landlords. However, this is actually not a bad thing because it will stop rogue landlords who have unsafe and inhumane multi-lets and filters them out, leaving us professionals to do it properly.

Article 4 zones are areas where the council has decided you can only buy existing HMOs but no longer set up new ones, so this is another thing to check before buying any HMO. You will also need to inform your mortgage broker if you are intending to rent the rooms out individually and make sure that you have the correct mortgage in place.

Keep it simple

A good multi-let that will be worth your while should have at least four lettable rooms with a communal lounge area (see diagram below). Rather than renting out the whole house to a family, you simply rent out each room in the house. You don't actually need a communal area, but unless the bedrooms and the kitchen are very large I would always recommend having an area for housemates to dine.

On the next page is a typical example of the layout of a good 4-bed HMO.

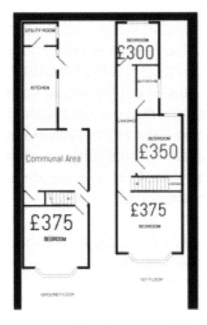

Total Monthly Rent = £1,400

I used to think that to do this you must find a large 4/5 bedroom detached house with a great big driveway for all the cars. You would also need a huge kitchen with spacious hallways built in and, of course, en suites in all the bedrooms. On top of that, don't forget all the planning permission and building regulations to comply with, along with an HMO Licence.

By the time you have done all this, on top of your deposit money, it would probably cost £50,000 for the conversion, along with six months' worth of work and planning.

The reason I thought this is because that is the impression I got from investors who were already investing in HMOs. I have noticed that often, when people are successful at something, they deliberately overcomplicate it and make it sound harder than it is. I'm not sure whether it's to make them look clever or to scare off the competition, but whatever the reason, I've seen it time and time again.

I'm about to take great delight in exposing all the myths around HMOs and giving you the absolute truth as to how you can get crazy high returns and become financially free by investing in as little as three properties.

The builder lied to me

The first time I found out about HMOs was when my mentor was buying one back when I was a teenager, as I mentioned in Chapter 1. We'd become friends with a builder whom we will call Chris. Chris specialised in HMOs and he really seemed to know his stuff.

My mentor was on track to buy a 5-bed HMO in Birmingham that was in a bad condition and needed knocking back to the brick. Chris would do the conversion and I would subsequently manage it. I was doing this purely for experience.

I remember having a meeting with the two of them and Chris was explaining how important it was to have an en suite in every room. He said,

"Unless you want scumbags in your house, you absolutely need en suites in all of the bedrooms."

Chris also told us that buying a property in good condition was silly because you would pay over the odds for it. It was much smarter to buy a cheap run-down property and add value to it. Looking back, it's obvious that Chris just wanted more money for the works, but at the time it seemed so convincing and right.

My mentor paid £125,000 for the house and in excess of £50,000 for the renovation. His total investment came to approximately £81,250. I rented the property out for £1,750 per month. The rooms were small and the en suites were crammed in. This is not a bad investment, but when discovering a little more about the industry and waking up to the builder's lies, we could have done a lot better!

Five shocking truths about HMOs

I didn't like the house very much, but my mentor had asked me to fill it with professional tenants. This was a great practice run for when I had my own. I was going to take this seriously and learn all I could. In my mind, this was my property right now!

By the time I had rented out this 5-bed HMO I had learned some million-dollar lessons. I was using a website called spareroom.co.uk and every day I would phone prospective house-mates, show people around the property and get their feedback, as well as constantly check the competition in the area to see what the rental fee was for other HMOs.

I noticed something very strange.

1) Finding tenants is easy

I had assumed that it would take a month or two to find a tenant, and then they would need an-other month or two to move in. Filling a whole house would surely take three to six months? I was wrong!

I filled the whole house within six to eight weeks.

Every single day new prospective housemates would be posting on spareroom.co.uk asking for rooms. I would call them and they would want to view and move in almost immediately. I charged an admin fee to the tenant of £90 and that was my only commission. The landlord was getting a free tenant finder – me – and I was learning loads.

The tenants were never local, but were relocating for work reasons from all over the country and all over Europe. They were young professionals wanting to focus on their career for a few years, while saving as much money as possible for later in life. They had a choice: they could rent a small apartment for about £500, plus pay their bills of around £200 which would total £700 per month just for a roof over their head. The other option would be to move into a fully furnished room with no hassle, with all their bills paid, for a total of around £350 per month.

Some tenants may prefer to live alone and pay a lot more, but a very large percentage would jump at the opportunity to save more money and have the hassle-free houseshare.

For these reasons, finding housemates was easy.

2) En suites are poo

When looking at some of my competition offered from other landlords I saw some really bad rooms. The thing that really surprised me was that many of them didn't even have an en suite so tenants were expected to share a bathroom, sometimes even between four people. I then remembered what Chris the builder had said,

"Unless you want scumbags in your house, you absolutely need en suites in all the bedrooms."

Although some of my rooms were small and awkwardly shaped, I was proud that they were all en suite. I began to notice that prospective tenants were not paying any attention to the en suites or asking about them before viewings. They would be more interested in the speed of the wifi, the nearest bus stops and whether the bedding was included. I slowly came to realise that many housemates were not as bothered as I thought about en suites. I did a survey with over 600 tenants and some of the results I found were astonishing.

On average, a housemate will pay only an additional £35 per month to have an en suite.

Guess how much they would pay extra to have super-fast wifi? Also about £35 per month.

To find a house with space for en suites in every bedroom you will pay more for the house. Then to have them fitted you will probably pay another £8,000 easily. Yet your extra rent would be the same if you just paid £25 per month for super-fast broadband. Interesting isn't it?

En suites are not bad, but are massively overrated. I have found that housemates will usually happily share one bathroom between four people.

3) Centre sells, rural smells

I showed a 22-year-old lady from France around a property. She had just moved to Birmingham to start a new job and had contacted me about my rooms. I met with her at the property and she spent less than ten minutes looking around, said she loved it but had two more places to see and would call me later that day.

I naively waited for her phone call which, of course, never came. The following day, I decided to call her and find out why she hadn't chosen my house as I was determined to learn all about my customers' needs and do my market research. She told me that it was a little too far out from town. She had decided to move to a room that was more expensive but much closer to the centre. It turned out to be a place called Lozells. I was shocked! Lozells is very close to the centre but is infamous for its bad reputation and high crime rate and the houses are much cheaper to buy there too. Although my room was a little further from town, it was in a much nicer area, but she didn't care!

I had naturally assumed that the housemates would want to know all about the area. The history, crime rates, nearest parks and the nearest place to have a picnic. I couldn't have been more wrong. The only thing they cared about when it came to location was, "how many minutes will it take to get to the centre?"

4) Convenience beats common sense

As well as asking tenants why they didn't take my rooms, I would also ask the ones that did, "why did you choose this room?"

Their answers varied but always came down to one thing – convenience.

The obvious convenient thing they desire is a place that is close to town. Fortunately, my rooms were all very close to the Bournville train station so despite being a few miles away from the centre, it was still an easy and convenient commute. Never expect housemates to drive because they rarely have cars.

The other reason that they gave was that the house was furnished. Most multi-lets are furnished, some moreso than others. My kitchen had cutlery, pots and pans. The bedroom had bedding and nice pictures on the walls. The communal lounge had a coffee table and a nice television. This made life so much more convenient and comfortable for my housemates so they were prepared to move in faster and pay more rent. Purchasing cutlery, bedding, a TV and a coffee table cost, in total, around £250, but will ensure that I fill my house much faster and will bring in a total extra rent of around £100 per month. That's a 400 per cent ROI and it's all because of convenience!

5) You don't need a refurbishment

The first house I bought was also an HMO. It was located very close to the one I had been managing. I didn't bother with en suites; neither did I bother with a renovation. This property was just over two storeys so I didn't need a license and it had three bedrooms and two reception rooms. When a property has two reception rooms, I translate that as one reception room and one bedroom. Of course, when converting a reception room to a bedroom, you need to have your builder out, right? Wrong!

In order to convert a reception room to a bed-room, you need to put a bed in it! It really is that simple. All that needed doing was small cosmetic work. No builders, no knocking back to the brick, no en suites, just me and my mum!

My mum and I cleaned it, painted it and had it ready as a multi-let within two weeks and it cost less than £2,000. I then rented it out the rooms for the same price as the previous landlord's house that I had rented out, and within one month four professional tenants were paying me £1,400 per month in rent.

I had bought the property for exactly £100,000.

Case study
Purchase price: £100,000
Rent: £1,400
Deposit: £25,000
Bills and insurance: £300
Legal fees: £2,000
Mortgage interest: £220
Refurbishment: £2,000

Total investment: £29,000
Monthly cashflow: £880

Return on Investment is 36 per cent per annum.

It was actually an infinite ROI for me because I structured it as a No Money Down Deal, but we'll get on to that later.

Find the right mortgage

Many small multi-let properties are just residential houses and you would struggle to get an HMO mortgage on them. At the same time, you would be in danger of committing mortgage fraud if you simply got a standard buy-to-let mortgage and then rented out the rooms without permission.

I am not a mortgage advisor so am limited in the information I can give, but what I would say is go and find a good mortgage broker who knows their stuff when it comes to HMOs and multi-lets.

I'm happy to give you the details of my broker if you email me at samuel@property-investors.-co.uk.

Tax implications

The more money you make, the more tax you will pay. It baffles me as to why people get so upset by having to pay taxes because as Jim Rohn says,

"If you want to walk on the pavement and not in the mud, then you need to pay your taxes."

In 2016, the government announced they were planning to change they way they taxed land-lords on their properties. The essence of the potential change means that landlords would not be able to claim their mortgage payments as a tax deductible expense. This has scared many amateur investors off, which is good news for the professionals. Let me explain a few things about these changes and potential implications:

1. The people who make up the rules are the ones who make money in property. With this in mind, there are always ways around any negative changes and loopholes to be found. In this case, for example, buying properties in a Limited Company makes you exempt from the tax change. Also, another change that people are not talking about is that it is now incredibly easy to buy through a Limited Company. Coincidence? Of course not. Where one rule changes for the negative you will always find another rule changing for the good to make a loophole.

2. If you are a lower-rate tax payer, this will most likely not affect you at all.

3. If you have HMO properties and stick to my formula of 'buy low, rent high' you have very little to worry about. The reason for this is because the mortgage payments are so low, not being able to claim them as tax deductible is not really a big deal. It may lose you a few pounds each month but the people who will feel it most are high rate tax payers with high mortgage payments and the rent is just covering it.

4. The new changes will push rents up. As many landlords will be forced to pay more tax, the obvious thing to happen is they will put their rent up to compensate. This will lead to rents being pushed up and more tenants needing houseshares and willing to pay a lot more.

These changes may or may not materialise, but the lesson from this is that no matter what the economy does and what rules the government in power stipulate, you will always be able to get rich from property.

CHAPTER 5

Professional deal sourcing

Where to buy?

The first HMO that I ever rented out was in Bournville. I went on to buy my own house, also in Bournville.

My plan was to keep buying there because I had been told that Bournville was the number one area in the country for HMOs.

When I started investing in property and realised that HMOs were a great way to get extremely high returns, when it came to areas, I only really knew what my builder had told me and I considered him to be an expert in HMOs as he had some himself and had converted many. From his teaching, this is what I understood:

"London is the capital city of England and is the biggest city in the UK so many people want rooms to rent there. The only problem is that house prices in London are so expensive that your return is very low. It would likely cost you £1,000,000 for a 4-bed HMO near the centre of London and although your rents would be very high too, your ROI would be very poor."

The second biggest city is, arguably, Birmingham, so there are still many people wanting rooms to rent there. The problem with Birmingham is that the north is cheap and tacky, the south is expensive and the middle is just apartments. However, there is this little village called Bournville that is just a few miles away from the centre. It has a train station and superb transport into town and is famous for its Cadbury World so has many people coming in for jobs. For these reasons Bournville is a secret goldmine area for HMOs and there are hundreds of people looking for rooms there, and just when you think it couldn't be any better, the houses are cheap too! So, Bournville is THE area for buying HMOs.

For this reason, I planned to only invest in Bournville. It was about an hour's drive from where I lived which wasn't too bad, and I planned to get a management team in the future anyway. One day, a friend of mine told me he was buying two 4-bed HMOs in Wolverhampton.

I was very concerned for him. He asked me to rent out the eight rooms and I told him that I couldn't promise to rent them out as they were not in Bournville, but I would do my best.

The time came when he completed the sale and was ready for me to market the rooms. He had paid £125,000 for each of them and they were in immaculate condition ready to be rented out. I put an advert up and began planning how I would find tenants in such a small city as Wolverhampton where I would have to persuade people to move in. Within a few hours of putting up the advert I had six emails from six prospective housemates. I couldn't believe it! I thought to myself,

"Wow! There are two areas in England that work for HMOs: Bournville and Wolverhampton!"

I rented both houses out within one month and the total rent was £2,900 per month! This was actually better than mine in Bournville! After finding out that both Bournville and Wolverhampton work for HMOs I decided to go on a mission. It was a mission to discover where else young professionals are looking to rent rooms. It didn't take long before I realised something quite incredible. People are looking to rent rooms . . . everywhere!

Five-minute challenge

If I asked you to name a city right now ... I bet that there are tenants looking for a room in that city today. The only catch is it does have to be in the centre of a big town or city, but that still leaves a lot of places. If you named a small rural village with sheep around, then no, it wouldn't work!

Remember, centre sells; rural smells.

On the Property Investors Crash Course, one of the exercises we do is to find live houses there and then. I go first to show how easy it is and then the students follow afterwards.

I decided to do an experiment which was quite daring one day. I asked one of the students to pick a city and I said I would find a HMO property in that city that would generate high returns. I would have five minutes to find the house and do all my market research on the valuations and rents in the area.

A student quickly volunteered, his name was Bill. Bill picked Telford, which isn't even a city, it's just a large town, but he chose it because he lives there himself. I didn't know this at the time. As it happens, Telford is not too far from where I have already invested, so I asked him if he wanted to pick another city. He said no.

Within five minutes I had found a 4-bedroomed property in the centre of Telford that lent itself well to a multi-let. It was advertised with an on-line agency at £90,000 and after doing some re-search it was clear that the real value was at least £95,000. It was very close to the centre and the rent would be £350 per room, totalling £1,400. It would need some fire doors, a smoke alarm and paint.

I didn't have time to go to the property but did have pictures and an address. We all went through this property and it ticked every box to be a HMO and Bill was amazed, but a little sceptical.

He asked,

"How do I know it would rent out for £1,400? It just seems too good to be true."

We made a dummy advert for the property online and moved on with the seminar. By the end of the two-day programme we checked the progress. We had three people within 24 hours asking for a viewing. At this point Bill was sure it would work.

I later had to tell the prospective tenants that the property was not ready and passed them to another landlord in the area who was very pleased with me, but what an incredible lesson for all the students there. I could see them all in the coffee breaks on their iPhones looking for similar deals where they lived. Four months later, I had an email from Bill. Since the Crash Course, he had viewed the property and bought it. He was emailing to say thanks, along with asking for my letting agents details. Wow!

Five-point checklist

There are lots to consider when investing in any property, particularly an HMO, but it pretty much boils down to five things.

Area

People are looking for rooms everywhere, but as I mentioned earlier it has to be close to a centre. Wherever there are centres there are offices, shops, people, jobs and a buzz. It isn't your property that is going to give you an income, but the people who live there.

I typically work on the basis that the property has to be located within 15 minutes of a town centre for those without a car. If it's in a quiet cul-de-sac five miles out of town, it will not work. If it's on a main road with regular buses that take you to town within ten minutes, you might be on to something.

Good condition

The mortgage company will not lend money for you to do the house up. If you have to spend a £20,000 renovation on the house, that could have been the deposit on another whole house.

The less you have to spend on the house the better, because then your money will go further. I usually expect to spend a few thousands on carpets and paint, and then legally you may have to make a few amendments to make sure the house is safe as an HMO. But please don't spend much on refurbishments unless you know you can pull your money out later. Another reason I avoid refurbishments is because everything always costs more than you plan and takes longer than you think too. Remember that every month your property is being worked on, you are losing rent.

Four lettable rooms minimum

I have thought about doing 3-bed HMOs, but quickly changed my mind after crunching the numbers. The first two rooms in the house typically will pay the bills, mortgage payments and management costs. Anything after that is your profit.

If you have only three lettable rooms, your profit will not be much. Five rooms is very good, but bear in mind you will need two bathrooms and possibly a license. Four tends to be the sweet spot in my opinion and all the rooms should be a minimum of around 70 square feet.

Power team

Make sure that wherever you buy, you have a good network in the area. Sometimes people say they will only buy in their area so they can do everything themselves. This is a terrible plan because you will end up with a rope around your neck rather than financial freedom.

In order for this to be systemised and run smoothly make sure you have, above all, a good letting agent in the area in which you're buying. Never get a normal letting agent to manage an HMO or you will end up managing the letting agent just as much as you would have to manage the tenants. Instead, find a trusted supplier that specialises in managing HMOs. I learned this the hard way!

Price

Do not spend more than £25,000 per lettable room. If the house is a 4-Bed HMO you should expect to pay around £100,000 and no more. For a 5-bed, then £125,000.
This of course, is a rough guide.

For example, if the house was a palace and you knew you'd get a much higher rent than £1,400 then that may be an exception. It is crucial to know that there is not a direct correlation between house prices and rents. A room will typically rent out for between £300 and £400 per month. This is the case if the house is in Bristol or Stoke-on-Trent.

A 4-bed HMO in Bristol may be £350,000, whereas in Stoke-on-Trent it is just £80,000. It makes sense to buy in cheaper areas as the rents do not change that much.

Agents or advertise?

Finding the types of properties that tick all of the five boxes is very difficult when you start off, but it gets easy in time. When I started off I used to buy from agents. I then became a 'professional' so would no longer buy from agents but instead would advertise and do leaflet drops. I then became seasoned and went back to buying from agents. Today, I find most of my deals from networking, speaking engagements and agents. The moral of the story is to never turn your nose up at agents because they have access to more motivated sellers than you could count.

In 2011, I became an estate agent just to make friends, network and get free training. I only did it for three months but I learned three things:

1) Most estate agents are not property experts, but sales people that happen to sell property.
2) Making friends with agents is very valuable because they do come across excellent property.
3) Having a real job is tough. Three months is more than enough!

I have also bought some excellent properties from deal-sourcing companies. This can be a great way forward and very time-effective, and it also mirrors how they found the deal. However, be careful because there are many bad deal-sourcing companies around that will wash their hands if the deal turns bad.

Don't reinvent the wheel

Most investors squash their passive income, buying in areas that they like rather than sticking to the template. They waste tens of thousands of pounds on unnecessary refurbishments and give themselves a headache dealing with rubbish letting agents.

Don't be like most investors.

After spending years doing market research on HMOs and surveying my tenants, I have come up with this five-point checklist. Please don't add a sixth point, such as "It needs to be close to my house, or it needs to have a pretty garden."

You can either be financially free and treat this as a business, or be comfortable and treat this as a nice hobby. When I started writing this book I was in California. As I write, I'm in a beautiful resort in Thailand. If there's a problem with one of my HMOs back in England, does it make any difference where it is in the country? NO! Because I have systems in place that enable me to have a growing property portfolio while also travelling the world.

If you stick to this template you will find that your Return on Investment works out at least 20 per cent ROI and you will be able to buy more houses and benefit from more capital growth.

I will find a house 15 minutes from any city centre.
I will find a house in good condition.
I will find a house with four lettable rooms.
I will find a house with a trusted power team in the area.
I will find a house less than £100,000.

CHAPTER 6

Lease Option Agreements

When I started out in property I had no money, no knowledge or experience and was too young to even get a mortgage. It was just before the brink of an enormous recession and everything was going against me. However, within 48 months I had accumulated a portfolio of properties that could have enabled me to retire for life should I have wanted to.

The biggest thing that can hold you back is yourself. In this chapter I am going to reveal how to make serious money in property, starting with nothing. This is good news for those who have little or no money or for anybody not able to get a mortgage. It is also good news for those with money, because these strategies will enable you to leverage what you already have and achieve incredible things.

They won't teach you

In 2008 when I lost my second property due to the mortgage company going bust and the lending rules changing, I was left without a strategy for buying properties with no money. Buying and remortgaging was no longer an option and I didn't have any money to put into my next deal.

I was recommended to attend a course about Lease Option Agreements (LOA). I had no idea what LOAs even were but was told that it was a new way to buy properties without any money.

I attended a three-day seminar and it was not what I was expecting at all. People were jumping on the tables shouting about how marvellous LOAs were and it was like a three-day party, but I didn't actually learn much about LOAs. By day two, I was getting a little frustrated, especially after paying good money to be there. On day three, I was then offered the 'advanced LOA training' where we would actually learn how to buy a house with no money.

I signed up to this advanced seminar and they did teach how it worked, but I was left with huge gaps and still had no idea how to actually go about finding on of these deals. I had a basic understanding of how it worked but nobody from the training was confident enough to go and find one.

Since then, through sheer perseverance and on-the-job training, I have managed to buy many properties using zero of my own money and have used LOAs very successfully. It is actually extremely simple and I have explained it to children who have understood. You will probably know more about LOAs after reading this short chapter than I did after spending thousands of pounds attending lengthy seminars.

The essence of an LOA is 'buy now, pay later'. In the same way you could buy a car but agree to pay for it down the line. You can do this with property and it is completely legal in England.

You agree to buy a house for a set price in the future and in the meantime function as the owner. The future date could be as long as ten years away. While operating as the landlord, you will benefit from the rent of the property. When the date to buy comes up, the value of the property will most likely have inflated considerably, a situation from which you will also benefit. Anybody can take on a property as an LOA, even if they have no money or credit whatsoever.

This may sound too good to be true, but thousands of investors are buying properties like this all the time.

If you're not in a position to buy the property, then you can pass it on to somebody else or you can hand the keys back to the original owner as it is a lease OPTION agreement not OBLIGATION. The original owner, however, cannot change his mind and is obligated to sell at the agreed time and price.

First, add value

In order to be successful you must always be adding value. Elbert Einstein says,

"Do not try to be a person of success, but rather a person of value."

When we add value, the success will always follow. Money is a certificate showing you have added value to people. With this in mind, how on earth is taking away somebody's house from them without paying a penny, adding value to them?

Surely this is taking advantage of people? Why on earth would any landlord agree to you doing this with their property?

These questions are good questions, but when you delve a little further you see that this is a win-win situation. Whenever negotiating a deal it is always a good idea to first put yourself in the shoes of the other party.

What if the owner of the property has a property that is worth £100,000 but the mortgage is also £100,000. The mortgage payments are £300 per month and they haven't got any tenants. They are struggling to pay the mortgage and want to sell the property. They are dreading the long and expensive process of going through an estate agency and they know that even if they sell it for £100,000 they will not be left with a single penny. This house is a rope around their neck that is causing them sleepless nights and they wish they could cut it loose somehow.

You come along and offer to buy it for £105,000. You will pay them in seven years' time, but in the meantime take over complete responsibility for the house and pay their mortgage. On top of that you will pay them an additional £100 per month as a gesture of goodwill.

Will they be happy? Of course!

They were going to be left penniless and they had the big job of selling the property. Instead, they will have all the hassle taken away, no estate agent fees, £5,000 above the asking price and £100 per month for seven years!

You will also benefit greatly. You will take on a property without paying for it, you will rent the house out for £600 and make a nice profit each month, and will have the chance to buy a property in seven years' time for a price that's seven years old so probably an absolute bargain.

You may ask, why didn't the owner just rent it out himself? There could be many answers to that question. Some people just don't want to be landlords. Maybe this man lived in the house himself and had just got divorced from his wife. He wanted to move on and sell the house but there was no equity in the house and the mortgage payments were high. There are a million different possible situations where a homeowner would benefit from being offered an LOA.

Find your seller

When you can offer a solution to a homeowner that will seriously help them out, they will still often get cold feet when they realise how much money you will make from the deal.

I once had an email from a distressed seller named Jeremy. He explained that he had bought a property for his son to live in, but his son had now moved out. Jeremy bought the property for £95,000 and his mortgage payments were £145 per month and his mortgage outstanding was £85,000 He had since moved away and let his son pay a cheap rent of just £400 which was giving him a small income of £255 per month, but his plan was for his son to one day buy the house from him.

Jeremy had broken rule number one of investing – never let feelings and emotions dominate the process. He had also broken rule number two – don't try to kill two birds with one stone when investing.

Jeremy never really bought the property as an investment, he bought it for his son to have a cheap place to live and hoped his son would save up and buy it. However, since his son moved out, Jeremy was now left with an empty property that was costing him £145 per month with the mortgage payments and he was terrified that the house would attract squatters. Jeremy was adamant that he didn't want to be a landlord because he lived too far away to manage the property so the only thing left to do was to sell the property.

The first thing I advised Jeremy to do was to rent it out, but he was adamant he didn't want to. I tried to persuade him. I explained how he could easily get £550 rent and he could employ the services of a local property manager who could find a tenant within two weeks. I kept pushing until Jeremy was almost red in the face with anger stating, "I do not want to be a landlord." Some investors would say I was a fool to do this, because Jeremy may have listened to my advice and I could have lost a sale, but my number one priority is to add value, not get the deal.

After having the property on the market for eight weeks, Jeremy had had one viewing, two no-shows, three cancellations and no offers. He was very worried and frustrated because his mort-gage outstanding was £85,000 and it was look-ing unlikely to sell for more than £90,000.

It was at this point that he emailed me asking if I would buy the property for a quick sale at £90,000.

The magic words

I could have quickly offered Jeremy an LOA and tried to take the property off him. But I didn't because this never works; it's all about timing and the order of how you do things. I exhausted the options first with these three possibilities:

1) Rent it out yourself

The first thing I advised Jeremy to do is to rent it out. He adamantly told me know but I tried to persuade him. I explained how he could easily get £550 rent and there was a property manager in the area that could find a tenant within two weeks. I kept pushing until Jeremy was almost red in the face with anger stating "I do not want to be a landlord." Some investors would say I was a fool to do this, because Jeremy may have listened to my advice and I could have lost a sale, but my number one priority is to add value, not get the deal.

2) Persist with the agent

The second thing I suggested to Jeremy was that he continued trying with the estate agent. I informed him that it was normal for things to take a little while but assured him there was nothing wrong with the property.

Jeremy seemed deflated with this advice and was hoping for something more. He asked me to make him an offer and ranted to me about his frustrations with the estate agent. He kept travelling for hours, just to have a wasted trip and a let-down viewer.

3. Accept a BMV sale

Lastly, I gave Jeremy a heavily Below Market Value offer. I offered to pay £75,000. Jeremy was not having this at all and seemed a little offended. I tenderly explained that I am an investor and this is my business; I need to make a profit. Jeremy seemed to be running out of options.

On this occasion I still didn't offer Jeremy the LOA, but instead we set a date to meet again after some thinking time. I wanted him to mull over the options and I wanted him to come to a definite decision on whether he would want to rent it out himself or not.
This is genius because after this process there is no way Jeremy would get cold feet and say he wanted to just rent it out himself when he realises how much money I will make.
Also, during this process we have had time to build rapport and I have demonstrated that I truly do care about Jeremy and have taken time to come up with many different options for him.

It's when we meet for our next conversion I offer an LOA. The first thing I do is review what we have already talked about. I then ask him if he is prepared to reconsider any of the previous three options, namely, renting it out himself, persisting with the agent, or accepting a heavy BMV deal. He's still not happy with any of the options and feeling disappointed that it looks as though the estate agent is his only hope.

Getting to this point is the hard part, the rest is pretty easy. You now have found a homeowner who would benefit from an LOA. You have exhausted his other options so he will not get cold feet after accepting the LOA. You have built trust and rapport with him. Time to seal the deal. Here is exactly what you say next:

"Jeremy, I may be able to offer you something like this . . .

"I pay you X (£95,000) for the property, but you wouldn't get the funds for another X (60) months. However, from immediate effect, I take over the mortgage payments and take over with complete responsibility for the property."

This way, Jeremy makes more money down the line, and gets to walk away from the headache of the house straight away. He hasn't got any equity in the property anyway, and any small amount he does have will be swallowed up in estate agent fees anyway.

Don't answer any questions

At this point Jeremy can see that this is logically the best thing for him to do. However, he has loads of questions. Jeremy is thinking,

"What happens if you go bankrupt? What if you miss a mortgage payment? What if you die? What if I die?"

The worst thing to do is answer Jeremy's questions. If you answer him it will sound like you are trying to sell to him and he will raise his guard. Also, unless you are an expert your answers will not be smooth and polished and this will also worry him. The thing to do is to say this,

"Jeremy, I have explained in principle what I may be able to offer. However, I am sure you have got lots of questions and need to think this over. My advice would be for you to speak to a solicitor who specialises in property, and have some time to think it over. Here is the card of a solicitor I know deals with this kind of agreement (pass the card over). Perhaps you could give me a call next week if you are interested?"

This is also absolutely genius and I have had to learn this the very hard way. Convincing somebody who is likely to be very risk averse to agree to a strange LOA contract is nearly impossible. However, if you leave it with them to speak to a solicitor here is what will happen.

Firstly, they will respect you and trust you even more for not selling and for doing things properly. Then they will contact the solicitor. Please note that this needs to be a solicitor who you know doesn't mind being contacted and who specialises in LOAs and wants the business.

Then what will happen is the solicitor will do all the selling. They will put the homeowner's mind at rest and answer all their questions. The solicitor is a credible third party who has no axe to grind, but, of course, the solicitor will give the homeowner peace of mind to go ahead.

Sign the dotted line

Jeremy emailed me again to say he had thought about it long and hard and had spoken with the solicitor who was extremely helpful. He was interested in proceeding. Bingo!

If I had got the order of these events wrong or had tried to answer his questions and sell to him, I would have lost the deal!

I then sent over a one-page agreement that explained and outlined the LOA arrangement. We both signed it for clarification purposes and sent it to the solicitors. The solicitors then drew up a legally binding contract which we both signed. I was then ready to collect the keys.

Jeremy has managed to walk away from his property that was causing him stress with more money and less hassle than could have been achieved in any other way.

I have a property that is renting out for £550 per month from day one, generating a profit of over £4,000 per year and I am benefiting from all the capital growth in the property without needing any money or any credit to do so.

This is just one example of how to structure a Lease Option Agreement, but I hope you now understand how simple it is. This template is the best way to find, negotiate and complete on a No Money Down LOA Deal.

CHAPTER 7

Buying houses with no money

At this point in the book, you'll probably be thinking one of two things:

1. This is so doable and I can't wait to get started.
2. There must be a catch; I can't imagine this working for me.

I want to urge you not to be the latter thinker. In November 2014, I remember watching two of my students working on exercises together at the Property Investors Crash Course. Both of them had no previous experience in property and were there for the first time. Both of them were the same age and in a similar financial position. Today, one of them is financially free and the other is in the exact same job with the exact same zero property portfolio. It's interesting isn't it?

I can write books, put on intensive property training programmes, scream all the property secrets from every rooftop and put my heart and soul into making you successful, but unless you apply what you learn, it will not work. Only you can determine your success and all I can ever be is a helpful tool and resource along the way. When I first went on a property investment course I had nothing and I am not special or even a quick learner, but still today I earn more money than I ever imagined possible simply because I have devoted myself to learning while applying what I learn. If there is a little voice inside your head telling you of all the reasons why this will not work for you, now is the time to squash that little voice and say,

"Thanks for sharing."

If your spouse, parents or friends tell you that property investing is risky and you cannot possibly invest with no money, respond calmly,

"Isn't that interesting."

The reason you are this far into the book is because you are not going to be an average person with average results. Most people have excuses for why they can't pursue their dreams further and state the reasons why obstacles have got in their way, but you are unstoppable.

Be daring

Dan had done some training with me and I had arranged for us to go and see some potential HMOs. Dan only had £25,000 which was just enough for him to buy one of the properties, but we had five to see. There were two HMOs that were excellent while three were just good. Dan wanted both of the two excellent properties but he definitely didn't have enough money to buy both.

Dan said,

"I have a great idea, why don't we buy one as planned, but then buy the second one on a Lease Option Agreement?"

I explained to Dan that it wasn't that simple. We only had one day together and securing an LOA took a lot of work and only worked in certain situations anyway. Dan was determined to at least try and dared me to have a go. I was not very excited about the idea but agreed to give it an hour's try.

We went to the second property and knocked the door. I asked the owner if we could have a chat about their situation with a view to making an offer, which they agreed to. It turned out that they had recently inherited the property. There was no mortgage on the property and they were asking for £120,000. They didn't need the money but, of course, wanted to make as much money as possible from the house.

Dan looked at me. I could see he was eager for me to pitch an LOA and secure it for him as a No Money Down Deal.

I slowly began to ask them the three questions. They didn't want to be landlords, they were not prepared to take a BMV offer but they were happy to try to sell it with an estate agent. I told them I was prepared to make them an offer, which would result in us paying them £138,000 for the property. They looked excited and asked me to explain.

I proposed,

"I may be able to offer something like this ...

We could buy the house from you for £120,000 which is what you are asking. However, we would need 36 months to pay you the money. In the meantime, we will take over the property and pay you £500 per month. This would accumulate to £18,000 on top of the £120,000."

Of course, they had lots of questions. Did I answer their questions? Of course not! I followed the process explained in Chapter 6 which resulted in Dan having a No Money Down Deal that he rented out as an HMO. The profit from this deal amounted to £700 per month and it gave Dan the option three years down the line to decide whether to complete the purchase or to just accept the £25,200 he has already made in rent!

This opportunity came as a result of Dan being daring. How many of these properties would you need in order to become financially free?

At the end of the term you could buy the property with the rent you had accumulated, or you could sell it on to another investor.

Be creative

I had a phone call from a friend named Keisha in February 2015. She said,

"Samuel, I know you teach people to buy properties with no money. I've just turned 22. I have no money and, in fact, I am completely broke. I have seen you are running a training programme next month and I really want to come but cannot even afford the train fare from London. Samuel, as a friend, do you think I should come?"

This really put me on the spot. If I said no, she could miss the opportunity of a lifetime. If I said yes, she could come and not be able to secure a No Money Down Deal and be left financially even worse off after paying the tuition and travel costs. I remembered my story and how people had believed in me, despite my limitations as a broke 17-year-old, and quietly responded,

"Keisha, you need to be there."

The following month I was preparing the training room and guess who walked in? Keisha! With a big beaming smile and excited, expectant eyes. We hugged before she explained to me her plans to help the needy with the money she made from property after this programme.

During the afternoon session on 'No Money Down Deals' we were practising Rent2Rents and LOA searching when her face lit up. She left the room to make a phone call. She later explained to the group that she lived in a 3-bedroomed house that had two reception rooms. She was renting the property for £700 per month, but she had the idea to ask the landlord if she could rent out the spare rooms in her house. I congratulated Keisha on her creativity and we all agreed that if she had the space and was happy to live with housemates it was a great idea to get some extra cash flow.

Within one month she had received permission and moved three people into her property. This was enabling her to live rent- and bills-free while saving up for her next creative deal!

What Keisha achieved was not complicated and many would say not a big deal. But for Keisha this was life changing and almost replaced her full-time income as a nurse. The lesson here is to not overcomplicate things and get creative.

Deals are everywhere

I regularly get asked to coach professional football players because they are earning a very high wage but aware that it will be short lived so they need to invest well. In order to protect their identities I cannot name names but I will tell you about one player, whom we will call Liam.

Liam phoned me and told me he wanted to buy some HMOs to build up a passive income for when he finished his football career. He received some training and bought four HMOs which was enough to generate him a good income for when he finished. However, Liam was fascinated with the idea of finding a Lease Option Deal. He thought it would be a good challenge and wanted to put my strategies to the test as it sounded a little too good to be true.

Liam was very busy with his football career so didn't have time to go networking nor the inclination to start advertising or looking for a joint venture partner. Instead, we drafted a short letter which said,

"Dear Home Owner,

I am interested in buying your house.

My name is Liam and I I have been wanting to buy an investment property in this street for some time and happened to notice you were selling. My ideal set-up would be a 'rent to buy' type scheme which would ultimately achieve you more money but may not be something we could do through the agent.

If you would like to contact me direct, I can be reached on 0000000 or email@imnotreal.com

I am in a position to move quickly and sincerely hope to hear from you,

Kind regards

Liam"

Liam put 50 of these letters into bright blue en-velopes and hand-wrote the addresses on the front. He then posted them out to 50 hand-se-lected addresses of properties that were on www.rightmove.co.uk.

Within less than one week, Liam had ten people interested in talking to him, that's 20 per cent. Liam filtered these down to three serious people who wanted to go ahead with the Lease Option Agreement.

Liam's plan is to keep one for himself and sell the others on as packaged deals for £5,000 each. He will do this exercise every quarter as a hobby and have a skill that has set him up to make an excellent living for life.

What is stopping you from doing the same?

Nothing.

This is a great example to show that there are deals everywhere, even on websites as basic as www.rightmove.co.uk.

Use other people's money

Earlier on, we learned how to find deals that generate a minimum ROI of 20 per cent and beyond. Imagine if there were hundreds of people who had tens of thousands of pounds and were willing to wire as much money over to your bank account as you wanted and could do it today.

If you asked for £50,000, within a matter of hours it would be in your bank account.
You could then buy as many properties and HMOs as you wanted as long as you gave the lender a 10 per cent return on their money and you could give them their investment back whenever you wanted.

Well I have news for you; this pretty much is the case!

I have people practically begging me to have their money. They have £100,000 sat in the bank earning them almost zero interest and the concept of earning a fixed 10 per cent is extremely attractive to them. This may surprise you, but I have never asked anybody to borrow money. I have people queuing up to give me their money, but instead of asking them I attract them. There is nothing more unappealing than a desperately broke person asking to borrow money for an investment. This is something that we spend more time on at our training programme, as well as the correct paperwork to use for any joint venture like this.

Let's imagine that you borrowed £30,000 from them and you then bought an HMO that earned you a profit of £8,300 per year. This is very realistic. After four years you could have saved enough to have paid them back and paid their 10 per cent interest and even have some left over.

But where would you be financially now? You would be making a passive income of £8,300 per year. You would have £30,000 equity in the property. You would have gained any capital appreciation over the four years and have an appreciating asset until your retirement. All this, and you didn't even put a penny in to begin with of your own money.

Imagine if you had not just borrowed £30,000 and done this once, but you'd done this once per year over the four-year period. You would then be earning £32,900 per year complete passive income and have £120,000 in pure profit equity. For many people this would be financial freedom.

I think it's now time to stop imagining and turn this into a reality, like so many of my students have already done.

CHAPTER 8

Now what?

Return on Investment

We have learned that this business is not about feelings but about formulas. In order to begin investing in property professionally you must get familiar with being able to work out the ROI on any potential deals. To work out the Return on Investment you need to know two figures:

1) What was the up-front investment you have to put down?
2) What is the annual cashflow or profit from this investment?

The annual profit is then divided by the up-front investment, which will leave you with your percentage of ROI.

On top of this figure you should hope to benefit from capital growth, but never bank on this because capital growth does not pay the bills.

Recycle your rental income

The next important formula I call 'Recycle the Rent'. This is extremely simple while incredibly powerful, but many investors do not do it. Recycling the rent is when you put a percentage of your rent aside for buying more investment properties. This percentage can be anywhere between 10 per cent and 100 per cent depending on how much you need the rental income.

Earlier on I told you about Liam the professional footballer. Liam has bought four properties in the last six months and is generating a good £3,000 per month in positive rental income. He has decided to put 100 per cent of this income aside for buying more investment properties. Working on the basis that £30,000 is enough to buy another property, and each property will generate £750 per month in positive passive income, here is what will happen if he continues to live off his football income and continue to put aside the rent for buying more properties.

Date		Number of Properties	Monthly Passive Property
Today		4	£3,000
after 10 months		5	£3,750
after 18 months	(8 months later)	6	£4,500
after 24.66 months	(6.66 months later)	7	£5,250
after 30.37 months	(5.71 months later)	8	£6,000
after 35.37 months	(5 months later)	9	£6,750
after 39.81 months	(4.44 months later)	10	£7,500
after 43.81 months	(4 months later)	11	£8,250
after 47.44 months	(3.63 months later)	12	£9,000
after 50.77 months	(3.33 months later)	13	£9,750
after 53.84 months	(3.07 months later)	14	£10,500

This is the power of compound interest. If Liam just recycles his rental income instead of spending it, in five years time he will have 14 houses that generates him £10,000 passive income every single month. What about if he continues to do this for another five years once again. Let's see.

Date		Number of Properties	Monthly Passive Property
Today		14	£10,500
	(2.85 months later)	15	£11,250
after 5.51 months	(2.66 months later)	16	£12,000
after 8.01 months	(2.5 months later)	17	£12,750
after 10.51 months	(2.35 months later)	18	£13,500
after 12.86 months	(2.22 months later)	19	£14,250
after 15.08 months	(2.1 months later)	20	£15,000
after 17.18 months	(2 months later)	21	£15,750
after 19.18 months	(1.90 months later)	22	£16,500
after 21.08 months	(1.81 months later)	23	£17,250
after 22.89 months	(1.73 months later)	24	£18,000
after 24.62 months	(1.66 months later)	25	£18,750
after 26.28 months	(1.6 months later)	26	£19,500
after 27.88 months	(1.53 months later)	27	£20,250
after 29.41 months	(1.48 months later)	28	£21,000
after 30.89 months	(1.42 months later)	29	£21,750
after 32.31 months	(1.37 months later)	30	£22,500
after 33.68 months	(1.33 months later)	31	£23,250
after 35.01 months	(1.29 months later)	32	£24,000
after 36.30 months	(1.25 months later)	33	£24,750
after 37.55 months	(1.21 months later)	34	£25,500
after 38.76 months	(1.17 months later)	35	£26,250
after 39.93 months	(1.14 months later)	36	£27,000
after 41.07 months	(1.11 months later)	37	£27,750
after 42.18 months	(1.08 months later)	38	£28,500
after 43.26 months	(1.05 months later)	39	£29,250
after 44.31 months	(1.02 months later)	40	£30,000
after 45.33 months	(1 month later)	41	£30,750
after 46.33 months	(0.97 month later)	42	£31,500
after 47.3 months	(0.95 month later)	43	£32,250
after 48.25 months	(0.93 month later)	44	£33,000
after 49.81 months	(0.90 month later)	45	£33,750

As you can see looking at this chart, after another five years of Liam recycling his rental income the compound interest has kicked in even more. Liam would now have 46 properties that would be achieving a passive income of £34,500. He would also be a self-made millionaire and set up to buy a house every few weeks should he so desire. This is the power of recycling your rental income.

This shows that anybody can get wealthy through property over time and is part of the reason why the rich often get richer, while the poor get poorer.

You may not want to reinvest 100 per cent of your rental income, that's ok, of course, but make sure you do have a set amount that you put aside each month ready for reinvesting. Also, never put aside what's left at the end of the month to invest. Put that money aside before you pay a single other bill.

Learn to network

Expensive advertising can be replaced with effective networking. The property business is actually a people business and the better your people skills, the bigger your bank balance will become.

The best people to network with in this business are landlords, estate agents and deal sourcers. On top of this you will also need a power team, or be able to plug into somebody else's.

Landlords

Landlords are likely to come across deals that may not be suitable for themselves, but perfect for you. For example, a landlord friend may be looking for 4-bed HMOs in Birmingham but only be interested in anything that was BMV. They may come across a perfect HMO that was in excellent condition for £100,000 that would generate 25 per cent ROI. However, because it's not BMV they aren't interested. If you had informed them of your criteria and they knew it was perfect for you, they would probably pass it on.

This is just one example, but there are hundreds of possible cases like this. Maybe they are a serial property hunter but don't really have the funds to move forward, or maybe they see two at the same time and are only in a position to buy one.

So, how do you network with landlords?

There are many possible options, but I would recommend joining a proper network and making friends with like-minded investors. In networking, you reap what you sow. In other words, if you expect things from others before giving anything of value first, you're a bad networker. The key is to always be thinking about how you can add value. One of the things that I personally do is visit landlords' associations and property networks to speak and share my story. Once I have spoken for an hour and given them lots of value and informed them of new and current strategies, they will be delighted to help me. This has resulted in me receiving lots of unwanted deals along with many other perks and, of course, gaining a great reputation in the property world.

Estate agents

The first person a motivated seller will usually call is an estate agent. Being friends with agents is extremely beneficial to your business and will win you many incredible deals. I have agents who will call me before they even have the keys to a property because they know it's a cracking house and I will buy it. The best way to make friends with estate agents is to buy from them. Once you have bought one or two, they will treat you like royalty.

The best ways to network with estate agents is to physically go into their branch if they have one and talk to them. Let them qualify you for a mortgage even though you will be using your own broker, because it shows them you are financially qualified and gives you chance to build rapport with them. Be up front and honest, but never be a know-it-all and listen to their advice. I am so serious about getting close to estate agents that I got a job as one for a few months.

This can be a slow process but could set you up for some great deals. I usually only work with about three per city, otherwise it can become overwhelming.

Deal sourcers

Deal sourcers usually spend 20 to 40 hours per week searching for good properties. These people are doing the job that you would love to do, but simply couldn't have the time.

What might take an amateur 200 hours could take a professional deal sourcer a mere two hours. Building rapport with some estate agents, viewing countless properties, deciding which ones to offer on, then negotiating a good price while doing all your due diligence and working out the ROI is a lot of effort!

Just being in contact with trusted, knowledgeable and professional deal sourcers is very good, but being closely networked with them is priceless.

I myself often package HMOs for other investors because you cannot buy everything you see, and I pass many incredible deals. I am sometimes jealous of how good the houses are but there can be a list of reasons why the timing is not right for me to buy. Maybe my cash is tied up, or I'm out of the country and haven't got access to my required documents fast enough or I've already got a couple going though and it would upset the lenders. I just have to remember that what goes around comes around and a big part of my mission is helping others to become financially free.

So the question is, how do you become well networked with deal sourcers? It's similar to the way you network with estate agents. The best way to make friends with them is to buy from them. I would always recommend starting small though, particularly if you have not had a first-hand recommendation. Never wire £40,000 over to a stranger even if they promise to double it overnight. Start with one small deal, and then wait to see if they deliver as promised. Over time, you will be able to build a strong and trusted relationship with sourcers and do more and more deals.

There are other ways to become well acquainted with them though without having to buy through them straight away. For example, let them know your exact criteria and show them your proof of deposit. This is always a good way to remain high on their radar.

If I've found a super good deal, I'll usually pass it to the people with whom I most network, those who have bought from me before, those who have just attended one of my training sessions, those who I know are in a position to buy, or simply people who are well connected with me.

Power teams

Your power team should include a mortgage broker, estate agent, solicitor, accountant, workmen and overseers, and a good letting agent.

The most important people in your power team are the letting agents. Managing bad letting agents can be as bad as managing tenants. I am happy to plug people into my power teams if they are investing in the Midlands, especially if I have helped find the property.

Invest in yourself

Property is the second best thing to invest in; the best thing is yourself. I would much rather have my property portfolio taken away from me than my knowledge. There is a pattern you will always find amongst successful people – they invest in themselves and are always learning new things about their industry. I continue to be around people who are smarter than me or who are doing better than I am. However, when you are starting out this is absolutely vital.

A friend of mine called Jas read up about property investing. He searched Google and read a couple of books before going out and buying his first property. Jas didn't really know what he was doing but was excited and keen to make some passive income. He bought the wrong property, in the wrong area, for the wrong price. To make things worse, the tenants who moved in were criminals and the house ended up being attacked and burned down. Poor Jas had not bargained for this and had a terrible power team around him who were not able to prevent this from happening. Today, Jas has educated himself and has surrounded himself with a proper power team and things are very different. However, if Jas had done this in the beginning he would have saved hours of time and thousands of pounds.

Melissa had read about Lease Option Agreements and had found a No Money Down Deal. Just days before taking it on, she fortunately came along to one of the Property Investors Crash Course I run and realised that her contract was incorrectly drawn up, even by the solicitor! This could have lost her the deal or she could have ended up with a court case on her hands.

Property investing is easy but only when you know what you are doing. You can either pay for your mistakes or for your training; one weighs tons and the other ounces. My advice would be to talk to others who are already successful, find a good training programme while taking action, and also take precaution until you are confident in the strategies.

I have shared as much as I possibly can in a short book, but if you would like to receive training from myself and be plugged into my power team, please visit **www.property-investors.co.uk** and I would love to help you in your journey to financial freedom.

Exact next steps:

1) Join a community. We have a Facebook community group called 'Property Investors with Samuel Leeds'. I would like to invite you to search for us and join.

2) Work out how much passive income you need and how many properties you need to make that happen. Write down your goals and make them clear.

3) Meet like-minded people. I regularly host 'The Property Investors Circle' where we have live networking events. If you can make a trip, I would recommend booking onto this or something similar.

4) Claim your FREE video series that I have put together which can be downloaded at www.property-investors.co.uk

5) Find out when the next Property Investors Crash Course is. Book yourself and loved ones onto this programme and watch your passive income explode. Details: www.property-investors.co.uk

About The Author

Samuel Leeds has helped thousands of investors towards achieving their goal of financial freedom. Being able to make complicated strategies become simple philosophies, Samuel has earned a reputation for being one of the most inspiring investors in the UK.

Samuel is the author of Amazons #1 Best Seller: *Do the Possible, Watch God Do the Impossible*, which has led him to speaking at churches and business conferences all across the world.

Training Kings was founded by Samuel and is currently the largest Christian Business Network in Europe.

To get in touch or to request Samuel to speak at an event please visit www.samuelleeds.com.

Here's What Others Say About Samuel Leeds

"I have been very impressed with Samuel's teachings and with the massive value that he brings."
- Simon Zutshi, founder of PIN

"Samuel Leeds has a massive heart to help people along with a ton of knowledge. Every time this guy opens his mouth people are inspired!"
- Blair Singer, CEO of SalesPartners Worldwide

"Samuel has helped dozens of people within our organisation with his excellent property investment and finance strategies."
- Clive Lewis OBE

"Thank you for helping me get my first few HMOs. I now work because I want to, not because I have to."
- Christian Ribeiro, professional footballer

"Samuel really is a remarkable human being. He has been there and done it, got the T-shirt and now has nothing but value to give."
- Julian Maurice, Property trainer

131

Get In Touch

Property Investors with Samuel Leeds
www.property-investors.co.uk

Training Kings, Christian Business Network
www.trainingkings.co.uk

Samuel Leeds' Office
www.samuelleeds.com

email: info@samuelleeds.com
phone: 07840 186258